T0149795

Tender in the Age of Fury

Rants and Raves for Brandon Pitts

"In the four movements of this piece I have used poetry from James Joyce's *Chamber Music*, Ezra Pound's *Ripostes*, and {one poem} by Brandon Pitts. To complement the texts by Pound and Joyce, I searched for an appropriate text by a living Canadian poet ... Brandon Pitts proved to be a most fitting companion."

> – Classical composer Adam Scime,
> from the "New Music Concert Series: Then and Now" concert program, explaining why he used Brandon's poetry as lyrics for his composition *Earth and Air II*.

"I've seen Brandon Pitts read once before—at The Beautiful and the Damned at Zelda's a couple of months ago—and it was so good to have the opportunity to hear him do a solo read, with a longer set, on the closing day of Art on the Danforth. And when I say, "read," it wasn't so much reading as performing – often by memory – his voice and body moving and shifting along with the rhythms of his words.

Pitts' work is visceral, political, irreverent, historical, biblical, romantic, vulgar and lyrical. And you really need to hear those words and rhythms."

> – Blogger Cathy McKim of
> *Life With More Cowbell*
> (https://lifewithmorecowbell.wordpress.com)

"At last, poetry in motion. You are without a doubt, a wizard of the spoken word. If poetry were water, you could turn it into wine."

> – MJD Algera, poet

"There is a new movement, a new style of Poet emerging in the city of Toronto. A movement I hope goes viral. Poets who are becoming the rockstars or our literary scene in every sense of the word. Brandon Pitts is one of these Poets. On the page and in performance, he fills the stage with a lyrical presence, oozing a sensual vibration of power in his chosen words. His voice an instrument... His poetry, images of his past, present and future [are his] songbook, his album, his concert... One particular poem does deserve that little bit of extra attention and accolade. Lot, a poem that affected me emotionally, leaving me in a breathless state, having me swing hard between anger, disgust and empathy for the state of human evolution. A modern expose mixed with religious icons, a society failing at making a better world. The last line of the poem, a powerful statement, 'We are defining our times' rings honesty and truth. Brandon has a video poem for Lot that is a must see. (https://www.youtube.com/watch?v=CnofSJfKiV0). Lot is a powerful, moving piece, that should be read and heard by all.

As a poet and writer, Brandon Pitts is defining our times indeed. He raises the bar to a level that we haven't seen in decades. A bar that should inspire other poets and writers to reach for."

— Blogger Carolina Smart,
from the June 2012 edition of
Lipstik Indie, the "Rock 'n' Roll Poetry Issue"
(https://lipstikindie.wordpress.com)

Library and Archives Canada Cataloguing in Publication

Pitts, Brandon, 1967-, author
          Tender in the age of fury / Brandon Pitts.
Poems.
Issued in print and electronic formats.
ISBN 978-1-77161-174-9 (paperback).--ISBN 978-1-77161-175-6
(html).--ISBN 978-1-77161-176-3 (pdf)

          I. Title.

PS8631.I882T46 2016   C811'.6   C2015-905088-X
                                              C2015-905089-8

Published by Mosaic Press, Oakville, Ontario, Canada, 2016.
Distributed in the United States by Bookmasters (www.bookmasters.com).
Distributed in the U.K. by Gazelle Book Services (www.gazellebookservices.co.uk).

MOSAIC PRESS, Publishers
Copyright © Brandon Pitts, 2016

We acknowledge the Ontario Media Development Corporation
for their support of our publishing program

We acknowledge the Ontario Arts Council
for their support of our publishing program

ONTARIO ARTS COUNCIL
CONSEIL DES ARTS DE L'ONTARIO
an Ontario government agency
un organisme du gouvernement de l'Ontario

We acknowledge the financial   Nous reconnaissons l'aide financière
support of the Government of   du gouvernement du Canada par
Canada through the Canada Book   l'entremise du Fonds du livre du
Fund (CBF) for this project.   Canada (FLC) pour ce projet.

 Canadian   Patrimoine   Canadä
         Heritage   canadien

MOSAIC PRESS
1252 Speers Road, Units 1 & 2
Oakville, Ontario L6L 5N9
phone: (905) 825-2130

info@mosaic-press.com

www.mosaic-press.com

Tender in the Age of Fury

Brandon Pitts

mosaicPRESS

Contents

Foreword

Brandon Pitts

I went to a coffee shop to attend a spoken word event. The proprietor of the shop was asked to read something of his own work after all the other featured performers had finished. I was prepared to leave as the droning of the other writers had lulled me into semi-conscious state of boredom.

He got up, read two short pieces and smiled to a splatter of applause.

I was surprised.

Surprised at the rest of the audience that did not recognize this unrefined diamond that was buried in their midst.

I approached him after most had left, showed him some back issues of the literary magazine that I publish, and asked if he would like to send me a poem or two for the next issue. He sent two.

I read them . . . and recognized a poetic soul. Not someone who writes words in a stylistic manner, or words that rhyme, or words that amuse, but someone who has the soul of a poet, someone who lives poetry, someone whose life is a poem.

I took the two poems and suggested a minor edit, removing the last line of one poem in order to leave the reader with a sense of the infinite. Like a spark of magic, his eyes were opened to the possibilities of the impossible. It was like the awakening of Rumi, the catharsis of Blake and the annunciation of Yeats.

The poet that slept within was brought forth, and the words began to flow, crashing down upon the blandness of the herd like the parted waves commanded from the staff of Moses.

Now, I purposely use that biblical image because the poetry of Brandon Pitts encompasses the spirit of man, and the majesty of God. There is a divine spark within him that reaches for the heavens, dwells in the abyss, and breathes with the thunder. His knowledge of metaphysical and philosophical thought is braced with an experience in religious and spiritual practice. This all combines into poetry that is esoteric in nature, but speaks to the inner essence of souls that search for meaning in their lives.

When you hear Brandon recite at a spoken word event, the audience doesn't just listen, they participate with an opening of their being, an acceptance in their hearts, and an acknowledgement of their minds. They are captured by his words like a guru mesmerizing his followers.

Make no mistake, this is not a trick, a flash of spotlight or pyrotechnics by some illusionist of reality. People love his work because he is the mirror in which they see themselves, or what they aspire to be. His poems describe the inner essence of what some people are, those called the enlightened, and what many are not, the ones who search for an answer.

Is his poetry the answer? No.

His poetry is a call to search, and his poetry assures them that there are answers to be found.

Norman Cristofoli
January 4, 2013

Introduction

This second collection by Toronto poet Brandon Pitts extends the themes found in his collection *Pressure to Sing* (In Our Words, 2012), and provides readers with a clearer understanding of the interconnected personal, theological and political themes that run through his work.

Pitt's previous work may have left the casual reader somewhat perplexed and in search of a cultural "key" in order to fully appreciate it. Yet the fuller treatment in *Tender in the Age of Fury*, with the juxtaposition of erotic, apocalyptic, religious, political and cultural references, provides a clear intellectual parallel, and perhaps even kinship, to some of the key ideas and thinkers of the Renaissance.

For others, Pitts' point of view might recall the "Ancient Astronaut" of popular speculative literature in the late 1960s and early 1970s (of von Däniken, Pauwels and Bergier, Robert Charroux, Jean Sendy, etc.), and the links that this "flying saucer" enthusiasm had with the Cabalistic and Hermetic sources found in the nineteenth-century "Occult Revival." Though later "ancient astronaut" authors were clearer about their intellectual debt to Cabala and Hermeticism (in its alchemical form), they all had the common denominator that courses through *Tender in the Age of Fury*—an anxiety about the meaning of life in a materially and spiritually chaotic society.

A scion of the U.S. West Coast counter-cultural scene of the '80s and '90s, and the Toronto poetry circles of the present century, Brandon Pitts' work channels the tradition of "fallen angelic metaphysics" against the background of personal experience, economic globalization, and the Information Age trivialization of human thought to form an almost apocalyptic-Gnostic Utopia. Pitts returns the reader to the Hebrew/Christian/Islamic story of angels and men (and women) that is at the root of the modern consciousness, offering an immanent critique of its latest manifestations (as Marx criticized Hegel), so that he can say:

> *Right here*
> *Right Now*
> *we are defining our times*
> — "Lot", V

Terence Barker,
Toronto, Canada
November 11, 2013

To Rebecca,
Whose love gives me the strength to survive being
tender in the age of fury.

To Nik Beat (RIP),
Sublime poet and absent friend. I would hand you the
laurels were they but mine to give.

Legba
The Prophesy of the Coming Mannish Child

Artist's Statement

Though this section of poetry can be read in a literal sense, it is better understood as a series of allegorical symbols. I have sought to construct verse that symbolises the human movement and habitation on the American Continent. To deepen this symbolism, I have used some of the many facets of the American voice and the demonic side of American folk spirituality. This language, combined with the pulse and meter of a folk spell, creates a poetic grimoire for the American experience as it moves from east to west like a virus while drawing comparisons to the contemporary socio-political environment.

Kennewick Man

Crow
            silence

           so thick
I can hear heat rise from the desert plane

where the jarring scratch
of the sunbaked beetle
points me north

to sequoia
     and snow capped giants

to river's flow

and my time of dying
     the dawning of calendar days
until a burning need from the east
seeps through the land

     to pull me from the water
     so souls with good intentions
can pick at my weary bones

Delilah Went Cold

I.

beware of the Drubby
that wanders the cornfields at night

steals the souls of sleepers
and drives them back to the time

where men ate raw meat
and gnawed on dirt covered roots

tore at women with a brute fang
        proof . . . . of the love that a man can feel

Jim
        why'd you do that evil deal

back in the woods
where only the frogs heard poor Delilah cry

hey Jim
        can you tell my why

'fore that devil takes you
        casts you back upon the wheel

where Legba presides over the cycle of reason
        to purge your ordeal

II.

in the lesson of transformations
    where I sat on the wet nurse's lap

she sang songs about the old times
    in that far off land

where cracked hands
    beat spells upon drums

and how to sell your soul to the Drubby
    out on Highway 61

when he taps you on the shoulder
    take the deal . . . . don't look back

and the grimoire will reveal its secrets
    even to those who can't understand

    but it was droppin' hail
when I came to the crossroads of my life

down in Beauregard, Mississippi
    out on route 49

so I gwon thru the thistle patch
    contract in my hand

drew a circle in the cornfield
    where they go and see the Drubby man

III.

hey Jim
  why ya lay down yer plow?

hey Jim
  left yer woman to fend fer the sow

Jimbo
  gone to revel in the city swell

  but stopped to steal peaches
an' asleep in the hay

  they'll find you Jimbo
  find you one day

but tonight . . . you'll hop a freight train
  dream of new lands

where money and women
  come to a man

with the strength of dreams
  and the mind to foretell

but there'll be no more wishes
  from the Drubby's secret well

and this . . . was the prophecy
  that the angel foretold

a mannish boy would be born
  on the eve . . . . Delilah . . went cold

7

Ergot in the Rye

when the fog settles on the field
as the Forth Wind slows
        mice will scratch patterns
on church floorboards

and the spirit that silences birds of the tree
will push the sow down . . . deep into the sty
        on the day that neighbors can no longer plan
        their means
to the cycles of the moon

but a man can lean on the bible
smoking nightshade from a cob bowl
        standing minister over the mandrake
as Solomon had mastery over the jinn

until his children catch Saint Anthony's Fire
and misbirths plague the pure
        running widdershins
with eyes glued to the steeple

        and the Goodwife
        . . . buried in the yard
                was burned for black charisma
        and blind incantations

        Matthew approaches her headstone on the right
        . . . departs the stone from the left
                taking with him
        that damp cold that puts infirm into one's bones

for frost will soon come
to those of us
        who sustain our provender
through the mercy of the field

Aux Arc

ghost of Appalachian mysteries
      Adirondack peaks
running from Simon on the Delta
      past haunted deserts
to the land of Pixies

lo
      we are travelling to Eldorado
along the Buenaventura River
      where the Fairy King lords over gold
and souls are considered free

free of want
      and master's whip
      a plot of land
silver and ore

      have you heard?
we are travelling to Eldorado

Pox

in the beginning
    when dogs could talk
and children would touch bark
to feel spirits in trees

there came from among us
    a small boy
whispering futures
    of omens and reason

    they say his mother
had never known man
    and the boy could hear instruction
from elders long past

so we listened
when he told us of times ahead
    where a strange creature
would appear on the plain
to carry us vast distances
    places we'd never been

he said the beast was not to be feared
    but the pale man
who rides on its back
holding weapons that spit fire
    would be our undoing
so we rode those creatures
    some called horse
in search of a leather bound book
known to be the pale man's source of power

traveling the plains
    looking for its magic
until we came upon the village
of our enemy

we found nothing
    but tee-pees
full of dead Comanche
    their skin pocked with red marks

we knew then
    that the boy
who spoke with departed shades
was a prophet of things to come

so we called him
    Sweet Medicine

Volunteers

I was there ...

when the Reverend Chivington
    whisky on breath
and pistol on pulpit
sermonised from the Book of Joshua

filled with Holy Spirit
we marched upon the savage camp
as they waved Old Glory
in cowardly surrender

running in terror
we drove them down
    slicing flesh to save ammunition
chopping squaw and cutting papoose
    tripping the elderly
saving scalps and fingers
to trade for drink
in Denver saloons

the mannish spirit
forcing my hand
to burn tee-pees
making way for rail
paved road and commerce

    I was there
when the Reverend Colonel said,
"nits make lice"

The Doctor of Theology

for Roger Ailes

oh massa Ailes
why has it been forsaken
        Hosanna
and her sweet rosary bead?

dadgummit
the full custom gospel
        that you delivered
told us we were free

gone
was the solid sender
        sweet pretender
and the "good news" deceit

for the chillin of Gabriel
heard it in a parable
        while picking
in the fields of machine

why do you dance
at the misery ball?
        Can you tell me
my doctor of theology?

Tecumseh

down that yonder road
beyond the plough

where rows of peach trees
line the avenue at Five Points

Cousin Bud likes good company
heard a y'alls Southern hospitality

where all are welcome to the table
 ('cept the negra field hand)

now Maple's got swank
Cornelius Riley can predict numbers

and the diggers who tapped into y'alls well
wear the latest trousers

but there were those men 'n' women
who wore slacks pressed to the swell

who wanted to go to Clarksville
got held up in Austell

 maybe I'll drink 'shine
 down in Bowlin' Green

Lake Charles to Biloxi
Cornwall to Shawnee

Athens to Nazareth
she throws her golden ball

Eris, goddess of chaos and discord
why hath thou forsaken me?
did we not vow
to see our former selves on the other side?

now the seed of wolves
churns in my blood

and the clots of clay
were formed in defiance from above

so remember past loves
whores in the saloon

who got caught up drinkin' Sterno
discarded signs of the moon

tonight I walk with darkness
tonight I walk depressed
for the Lord join in my disdain for Georgia
till I marched all the way to Memphis

Sherman

and these
will be the causes of death:

bombs shall rain
torrents of hot metal
shot from cannon
pushing the campaign
through the centre of town
leaving the street
a passage of mud
along rows of hot cinders

we will press down on you
plantation owners of slaves
for we noble souls are prepared to die

your soldiers
addicted to morphine
will be saved by our heroine
to replace legs that will not sprout
from severed stump

then agents from the north
        yankee bulls
will follow the caravan
to gnaw on the carnage
like carrion birds
in camel hair jackets

for the righteous always prevail
and conquerors write history
    see we both lay claim
to that felled orchard
    but it is we
who hold the franchise
on the eve of these wicked days

and those beaus
who came to manhood courting
will be gunned down in their prime

    'cause we all know the belles with the large
    curls
        cradled by their mammies
    curtsy in hoops to hide the fact
    they's nothin' but harpies

see, you ain't right with the Lord
    and like that dark angel
who hath possession o'er the death bed
    my army will force you down
           into that fiery ditch
      where all accounts are rendered

The Hymnal of the Ghost

preacher tell me rightly
    will I go to hell

I have slain my brother in battle
    to the offending brigade's yell

we have seen them in the hour
    with their backs to heaven's door

        surely all are equal
            to die before the Lord

mother tell my rightly
    will the bell be rung by Christ

are we the rivals of history
    is God on our side

will the truth rain down like shrapnel
    to drown us in the storm

        surely all are equal
            when flesh falls from bone

so we hoisted up the standard
    to the hymnal of the ghost

cavalry on horseback
    infantry on foot

when mortar slams the hulls
    of iron clad boats

        surely all are equal
            in the agony of war

The Confederate

in my one-hundredth year
    I lived on a green hill
in West Virginia

weak in bone
    with seeping spirit
I melted into the landscape

ignored as I was useless
    my sallow flesh
gave way to an ashen complexion

what will I leave
    a stone effigy
a lifeless reminder of what I used to be

overlooked in the folio of classic texts
    scribed by literate negroes
who burned candles in Carolina shacks?

soon I will need a burial
    a hole
dug by old slave hands

who plucked the grains of Zander
    and share cropped his lands
in the fields of machine

    a memorial
    so my spirit may live on
in infamy

The Prophecy of the Coming Mannish Child

I.

and the angel came
as my ma lay bruised and beaten

whispering futures
    of omens and reason

a man-child is comin to you
in two-hundred-seventy-one days – minus a night

folks buried her in potters field
as it rained ice from on high

so this is how Delilah
    met ol' Jim

    fleein' from the overseer
who run the cotton gin

    couldn't stand
another day of abuse from his hand

some men hurt
    what they cannot have

but her wish for me
was to see her mannish boy free

    Lord, she ran from the plantation
    Lord, she tripped in the night
    Lord, she prayed like Moses
    that her baby child might survive

Tender in the Age of Fury

for I was born to a dead woman
out on the tracks

as crops were burnin'
and her killer stood o'er her an spat

    so the undertaker can put away his shovel
    'cause I'm standin' free

for I chose to be in this body
when the parsons is preachin' that the body chose me

I'll sun myself with the lizard
shed it like the snake

spit fire till it turn to money
lure the Drubby with a witch's cake

II.

castrate the pigeon
        hit on the road

lickin' the back
        of the psychoactive horned toad

vermin in conflict
        and the skeeters buzzin' tight

harvest moon a hauntin'
        Church . . . of the Toad of Light

Jim . . . accept your fate
        it's a bible truth

'cause you chewed the cactus
        drank its juice

ate its buttons
like a rough swallowed root

        now you run
from the lawman's lash

with beads of mescalito
        sweatin' out your back

III.

farmer shoo'd you with a shotgun
    buckshot follow you off his land

and those blood stained pants
    mark you a guilty man

    on good terms with the sheriff
    you'll find work with a gun

    but they'll find you Jimbo
    hunt you as you run

so you rode your horse
    till its shoe stepped on a diamond back rattle

then you was left
    to carry the saddle

to the Republic of Texas
    where they hand out citizenship if you're
    willin' to fight

    hallelujah!
as you vanquish . . . Iljii the Hind

    now Jim . . . this magic of the mountain can't
    save you
    the Drubby only answer one wish

    from Aux Arc shack
    to Adirondack witch

you're soul is young
but your body won't grow old

cause they're hunting you down
    for the day
        Delilah
            went cold

Zul Qarnain

there were three prophets in the east
     four prophets in the west

their words predicted the coming
     of my goat horn crown

and the enormous heap
     that was their temple

shall provide the stone
     for my vast wall

where archers will stand
     manning pots of hot oil

collected from the pits
     where it gushes forth from sands

in my domain
     the Occident . . . to the Levant

where murderous trolls
     push my phalanx forward

and fathers bid for the rights
     to my will over their daughter's bodies

I will take my pick
     one . . . for each mark of the rising sun

and Roxana shall be my bed-whore
     when the others cannot appease my lust

for she is my property
    as I have done unto them

and I will possess her
    like a foreign rock

after I have laid claim to her body
    I will build them a city

where the alter shall be built
    four and twenty cubits

six palms and twenty digits
    dimensions understood by priests

and those who worship Isis
    the sacred whore

but I cannot touch her
    until tribute is paid

and the golden coffers
    will be carried

by slaves
    marching behind my army

and their bibles that do not make sense
    will be added to my collective

when my forces traipse over their fields of grain
    as my generals delegate the storm

but wise men
    will aid in their reconstruction

with canals to move my ships
    and irrigate their crops

so their children can loiter in vast libraries
    teaching their parents

      and the future
          will be ours

our light will shine forth from a great torch
    seen for nautical miles

reaching beyond the places I have been
    and I will be remembered

for the fire that burns within
    will destroy this mortal body

and keep on burning
    radiating from the tombs to the farthest reach

haunting the Himalayas
    and the Syrian plains of Armageddon

to the rock in Plymouth
    and the pueblos of California

they will rush to bow before me
    for I am the vicegerent of heaven in this terrestrial hell

heavenly angel
    earthly devil

I am the Kingdom
    and I am Legba

Kennewick Man Again

Crow
on the hot asphalt pecking
at roadkill rising like the heat to
dodge the fast moving truck belching clouds
of spent diesel leaving the dung
beetle to crawl in circles on the festering
trash showing me the way to futility to clear
cut forests and suburban sprawl where dams
tame the Mighty Columbia

that's where I'm stuck

where I'll die

        forgotten

A Potion for Good Fortune

precious kernel
lovingly place the seed
    cover it
taking time to smell the hidden life
within tilled earth

an amphora of clear water
    space for sun and air

then wait the harvest
to feed the hunger
ours
is but a civilisation opposed to the grander thing
    a proper order

Crow is maligned

for he pecks on death

a situation that gives him patience

knowing that one day

      he will feast on us.

The Apocryphon

The Apocrypha

Artist's Statement

African American Slaves used to subvert gospel hymns and scripture to communicate among themselves in a way that the overseer could not understand. This was one of the earliest forms of Culture Jamming.

In this section, I have subverted religious scripture, gospel and apocalyptic scriptural stylings much the same way, creating political/socioeconomic allegories. This is achieved by juxtaposing the ancient with the contemporary to forge new poetic imagery with older artistic traditions.

The Apocalypse of Weeks

In seven visions.
For Pope Francis and the original Christians, dangerous people who
were thrown to the lions, and Canadian poet Nik Beat, for the day
he stood up to confront the priest before the entire congregation,
singlehandedly reclaiming the last vestiges of
Rock 'n' Roll.

Vision of the first

in the shadows of my sanity
where neurons fire static
and the mystical storm is wet with distortions
    the sun had just set
on the final millennium

o daughter of Irma
secret muse of my deepest cuts
destroying me with your grace
    can you see the tear that lies
– not beyond our vision –
but in the space where the eye connects to the
    brain

it is the tear that exists
on the bridge between dreams and insanity
where dumb messengers
walk in the field
    wolf heart psychics go for strolls
and the demented meet their phantoms

in this place
the shadowy veil is pushed aside
    not the veil that tickled your hand
as you touched a piece of the cross
that crucified Christ
    but that, of the lower curtain
home to apparitions who speak to you
as you hurriedly walk
past darkened cemeteries

it was out of this tear
in my waking consciousness
where emerged a chrome-shod stallion
    its coat, black as our eyes

do not lend it your money
    for on its back
rides the ghost of greed
and shallow dealings

Vision of the second

I hath seen the ghastly rider
    the one
who is marked by a swarm of hummingbirds
as he pursed his lips

his caste is uncommon
    he is the patron of criminals
men who steal lives
and abandon caring for cash

he dismounted
and slowly walked through streets
that were aligned
to the astral procession of the luminaries
and stood before the Great Seal
its copper corrupted and green
though its strong arm bore a polished shield

on the edge of the cityscape
before the ocean
with outstretched arms
he summoned his minions

out of the sea they came
the masters of all they envision
where I stood on the beach
like an urchin in envy
as they paraded their Nubian queens

it was on this corner
where I could see
my only option
was to accept their number of weeks
a counter to track my movements
as they provided for my every need

spirits on the left of me
forces to the right
I looked into heaven
where reality cracked
and the mystic hosts, the Chayot
returned running

and those angels of a higher form
kissed my lips
causing them to tingle
as the Ophanum hath forsaken
circling the fallen buildings
and the Elohim issued their warning:

there will come to you a man
with one eye
he will show you water that you cannot drink
    fire that will not burn
a warning to others
    he travels fast

as fast as the speed of light
and can appear in many places at once
and in as many forms
speaking all the languages
reversing the edict of Babel
he will survive the flood
fire and brimstone shall not harm him
for he carries with him a number
    an ISP, tattooed on his chest

Vision of the third

I saw the shallow rider
marksman of the holocaust
impervious to rain
as he stood above us on the knoll
making his presence known
    and the believers bowed to him in worship

he carried with him
a well worn tome
marked with the iniquities
of many generations

and the book was sealed
with twelve locks

the rider broke the first four locks
releasing dust
that smelled of sweet roses

he cracked
the fifth, sixth, seventh, and eighth locks
then came the smell of burnt sugar

upon the breaking of the ninth, tenth, eleventh,
    and twelfth locks
I could smell the revolting stench
of all the world's rot and feces

the rider opened the book
    within its pages
I paid witness to the horrors
of many sleepless nights
wandering through foreign landscapes
of concrete and asphalt
where the people
spoke in whispers and hisses

o daughter of Irma
it is you
who could save me
    taking my hand
and leading me
to righteous lands

do not leave me to the madness
of these streets
where I am tracked
by their banks
and marked with their ID
an ISP, number of weeks

o daughter of Irma
if you ever remember that you once loved me
you'll find me in the ocean
drowning
alone to the world
and peed on by the dogs of territory

    but know this:
        I will die unmarked
           and free!

Vision of the fourth

it was the happiest time
writing poetry
as the pristine daughter of November
lay naked
next to me in her sleep

she had been perfect
I could not ask for more
and for the first time in many years
    I had achieved mental peace

but the tyrants of fortune
would not let me rest
for these were the days
when the dead were not buried
but their souls held in a virtual stasis

o daughter of Irma
tender in your sleep
out of the sky came a white dove
with a pine sprig
balanced in its beak

it circled above us
as we sat among the financiers of sickness
where the painted slut of September
distracted us with her hypnotic ways
feeding the masses numbing hallucinations
and leaving them cursed with reality

Vision of the fifth

and there came
walking up the knoll
a lone sheep
who turned to the people and said:

while you were shopping
these men of means took control of your mind

they shaved our wool to make mufflers for their wives
leaving us cold in a seemingly endless winter
push down those senators
march upon that banker

will there be a place for us in their heaven?
we would certainly make room for them in our hell
lash marks upon my shoulders
as I ring the church bell

Vision of the sixth

spurred on by the sheep's words
a young man
stood from the crowd
to confront the shallow rider
issuing the challenge of the righteous

and the young man said:

on the senate floor
I will crush them
to their fall
o the night

rendezvous
with the fifth column
on the eve
Napoleon rides

Jesus called them shepherds
though God weeps for the sheep
don't let righteous men shave you
take cannon to subway and streets

shout! shout!
holler to the masses
or is your throat too numb to yell?
stand up if you feel cheated
topple the overlords of wealth

full tilt & spittin' fire
in my hand the new bible
sound out the custom gospel
delivered with a rifle

on the senate floor I will crush them
overturn their flank
take back the suzerainty I hath given
with my vote, I will reclaim

woe to them
in the smoke darkened sky
for now the people will be the drainer
on the eve Napoleon rides

Copernicus shall cast no shadow
the apocalypse of weeks
smash the walls of prisons
sharpen the guillotine

revolt!
revolt before they take control of your food
starve you into submission
numb your mind with glass tubes

we continually follow your pointed finger
though you have moved a thousand times
using fables as weapons
so black spots move about our eyes

where are we in the camp –
in the tent, by the fire?
put the priest on the block
chain the black friar

punish those who have taken from you
there are no nutrients in what you eat
the CIA cannot stop us
live hard, die free

drive to the crest to Calvary
take back the nickel and dime
arrest the politician
on the eve Napoleon rides

Vision of the seventh

there was a war on earth
fought with misinformation and taxes
waged by private firms
who owned public administration

> but what is
> is not what once was
> and does not have to be

so filled with the memory of the thinning
that exists around the Holy Rood
I prayed to the Lord of Hosts

and ministering angels
descended from heaven
to white wash the crowds with sense
infusing them with the ability to discern many things
        secrets . . . and harbingers to days of sweet nectar
peace . . . . and no more need for the bible trade

a life of Rosh Hashanah for you
Christmas for eternity
Eid Mubarak everyone
and salient blessings for all

Rapture

in the age of third helpings
the fat will fall from the vine
juices of plenty shall flow
and mugs will clash in salutations

gone will be the days
of impoverished dinners
and the second helpings of our fathers

I want to be served thrice!

fill my platter with rich foods
basted in butter

for in that age
the abundance will drip down my chin

Meredith Hunter Reversed
for Stedmond Pardy

like Woodstock
Manson
Altamont
    today I turn twenty-one

gone are the days
when felicity wore a flower in her hair
    now worry is worn
on sallow cheeks

"don't fret,"
they say
    "mother's serpents will attend to everything
keeping your bottle warm"

o daughter of Irma
    these trials cannot last
there will come a time of reckoning
where all will be reversed

knees bent to pray
    hands held to the sky
we will leave this shore
gone to sea on white sails

    our prosperity

A Poem for Aq

Why couldn't I have met you a long time ago
when the ocean was born and
the haze pulled me into existence from the fold

We could have been pleasure

And I would have said to you the word
and you could have taken from me
that life altering breath

Nimrod

Let them fill their church on Sunday
sprouting hymns to virgins
while others worship the clay toad
        they look at each other with misunderstanding
        for their efforts were confounded
                on the mound

Let them pray
as lightning strikes the steeple
while I worship in disaster
        the electric moment
        filling their hearts with terror
        as the Lord doth confound their efforts
                on the mound

Let them ignore the ringtone
as the cellphone vibrates across the table
like a planchet spelling out doom
        I will take pleasure in the storm
        Answer it...
and you too
        will be confounded
                on the mound

II.

They all love the antichrist
born into law and order
fuelled by rules and legalised crime
his name is Nimrod
and you are working for him

For like the Christian Saviour
he hath risen again to repatriate the people
swathing them in luxury
helping brothers and sisters of the world unite
in one national embrace
while leading them to believe that he teaches love
    and tolerance

But tolerance is to tolerate
and Nimrod hath provided one bar of soap to wash
    them all
so their skin will no longer smell of pheromones
and bees shall not molest them
until the day
his efforts
    shall once again
        be confounded
            on the mound

The Widow's Mites

the widow's mites
picking out lice
I find myself scratching on skin

turning the cheek
I bruise bent knee
what's the use in Divine petition

instalments pay on the mattress
where my enemy hides
deep within the folds

I'd heat my trousers
laying them out
but there's no coal in the stove

    oh, the widow and her mites
    two coins and a dead husband
can't save her

itching . . . . itching
the mites in my bed
brought in by the landlord's cat

it takes money to wash sheets
blood stains cotton
try not to pick at the scab

the bug bit the orphan
while the chevalier on the hill
kept his carpets pristine

his lowly maid
daughter of the widow
vacuumed out the box spring

    oh, the widow and her mites
    two coins and a dead husband
can't save her

Magdalene

for Rebecca Brooksher

in a stone garden I have sat
    waiting

I had visions of you as a child
    a dark madonna, sans the suckling babe

you would answer the calls of the priests each Wednesday
    in the evening . . . their time

then I travelled
    from the high country to the sea

to teach them religion
    and you no longer had to suffer their ways

now . . . your body will feel the touch
    of one who is rightly guided

and you will know that love comes
    from some other place

for when that daemon
    of self destruction

lies dormant and asleep
    you will hear whisper of your worth

then I will call you Magdalene
    and together . . . we will be

Into the Plash

I fall
entering the shadow
where reflections glisten
that place between thought and death
where dreams emerge from sleep
past and future meet
and heaven borders hell

it's the surreal space within a drop of water
not forward, into the wet density
but back
before the sound happens
moving in reverse
through my travels
within the reverberation
and into the plash

Lot

Thus were both daughters of Lot with child by their father.
(Genesis 19:36)

I.

There was a time
when I could separate
the sublime from the gross

But now each day
is to deny the arson

Scions of Isaac
Don't complain
We are defining our times

From Hedon to Hebron
I have heard the angels cry

And it is Alef
From the mouth of God
That unites

II.

I was once pure
but warmed a seat in the senate
Dope sick
The power of the penance

We smashed the idols
worshiped Yahweh
knelt in prostration
among the trees of Mamre

Essence filled our prayers
Melchizedek blessed us with wine
Fighting for Sodom's king
paid a purse full of dime

Then we traveled to the spot
where angels had fallen
There spoke the words
that raised up the golem

On the road to Haran
from rib made the sister
Woman for Prometheus
hellfire tempter

Oh to be young again
What would I redo or say
To touch her pliable curves
my hands moulding the clay

But it was all for naught
when Azazel kicked the sand
Saved my uncle's son
with the waters of Zam Zam

Quick, call the Rabbi
We need to kill the golem
Debauchery and shame
marked my days in Sodom

III.

Late nights
in Sodom and Gomorrah
But it was love
benevolent euphoria

Seven seconds to midnight
we heard the toll bell ring
Slave ship cometh
hung flesh with wings

Abraham, Abraham
Uncle, why?
You raised birds from the dead
released them to fly

The trumpet blast
the sinners sang
we spat on gold plated streets
broken from tribute to the king

Pulling out of Sodom...
and then broke the levee...
Backed away from the lake
like Sabbatai Zevi

Nowadays
I make love to two daughters
Seems I'm the only prophet
never saved by water

Cult of Isis
mushrooms and tithe
The idols watched
as her sweating body writhed

The evangelist
called my daughter a slut
But the orbs decreed
she was ruled by Malkhut

I left my wife
a pillar of salt
Bronze men, statues
glowing in glut

Now it's been so long since I heard
the sermon of the Sodomite priest
pushing comely angels
melting from the heat

Searing, searing
reach up to the heavens
Binah, Chockmah
swimming with depression

Lord I am sad
but I don't know why
lying naked between two daughters
yet I feel like I should die

We lay awake
waiting for the cosmic decree
as the Ten Sefirot of Nothingness
swell   and sing

I've gone unnoticed
my crimes washed complete
a respected patriarch
of the next two centuries

But who are you
to ask me what I've done?
Send your gripe
to the impotent congressman

The priests were wrong
the bible unwritten
Today I trade spice
with a heathen Egyptian

Daughters, oh daughters
can you ever forgive me?
But it was you two girls
who got me drunk and stripped me

Fire, Brimstone
order in the cosmic blast
The angels said, "Let there be ten."
but I was seven-tenths to the last

Oh you two daughters of Lot
on earth as it is in Hades
The next generation will be born simple
consumer subjects, incest babies

IV.

After 300 years
held up in a cave
the cult prostitute
foresaw the coming rage

Venus and Mars
remember the lash
Whipped men in temple halls
harem girl in a sash

Tifferet, Tifferet
Hod felt the splendour
I ignored the vile
focused on the tender

Bricked by Abraham
mortared by Ishmael
I had to pay tithe
to the great stone idol

Like Al-Uzzah and Lut
I loved those two sisters
so I moved the family to Iram
city of a thousand pillars

Down from the mountain
to the town of Qureshi
the Azan was called
but seven wives too many

Tent in the desert
mud wall in the town
pay taxes or go hungry
swim or drown

They took 360 idols
from the Ka'aba with pain
The gods were abandoned
     only Allah remained

V.

Right here
right now
    we are defining our times

Our ingenuity makes everything easier
There's no need to flex
Everyone's a musician, an artist
They are translating my opinion and broadcasting
    it to the world

We are all beautiful
all brothers . . . . . all sisters

I can go "green" with my compostable cup
organic with my lettuce
Corinthian Leather™ in my SUV
Fair Trade with my chocolate

They are reading about it in China
Searching it in Pakistan
Debating it in North Korea
It's going viral in Iran

I can record my every move and you can watch it
    in the cyber universe
adding a whole new dimension to the mundane of
    my day

I can comment on
"like" or "dislike" just about anything
Avoiding the cheesy
Downloading all that is "cool"
Post my profile

Tender in the Age of Fury

"Friend" you
"Unfriend" you
Change my status
Delete your comment

I can do it all
Be it all
Or just sit it out and order food from my house–
twenty minutes or it's free

For I have touched the sublime
Made love to the grotesque
My life is spent
Never to get up
Never to ascend

        Because

Right here
right now
        we are defining our times

John 2:13

Yeshua ben Joseph
bring them to their knees
demanding respect

strike them in retribution
leaving bloody welts in the place of entitlement
righting the wrongs
redistributing wealth by overturning the tables
as fallen coin echoes off the dome in the hall

Lash them my Jesus
strike their skin
bring down thine fire upon their backs
with your whip of chords
ignoring pleas for clemency and compassion

O dispassionate Christ
whip them with inspired arm
and leave them bleeding and poor

Smote them with thine Holy strap
so they turn the other cheek
ready for the second smack

Flog them Dear Lord
chasing them as they run

Sitting in the Senate, Listening to Council from Caligula's Horse

I put on the breastplate of Aaron
clutch my chest to feel the vibrating Urim
as the Thummim pulls my hand
like a gyroscope to a string

    it tells me what I should do

I shall lift the shield of Alexander
consult with Caligula's horse
who will whisper secrets into my ear
on how to breech the Levant
conquer Persia
and win your love

Hammurabi

I.

Riding forth onto the Sumerian plain
The hooves beat like drums
In tune with locusts
The Marsh Arabs sing
Praise to One God
  Swelter smears kohl
  Parasol protects
  Devil watches over the Yazidi
  The rest are governed
    By Hammurabi's Code

It was dry for those who prayed for rain
Until the lord of the sky brought the flood
The people did not believe
In burning the crops of my enemy
A curse on the homes of families
  Malaria killed the voycheck
  Deluge destroyed the Apkallu's city
  Soldiers used the ruins for cover
    The only ones standing
Were the strong

Ride; ride, out onto the plain of Shinar
Punishing my horse to continue
My chariot faces tomorrow
With the sun on my back
Bitumen brick, black tar mortar
Built the city four and twenty cubits
With lapis lazuli
Lining the ziggurat ramp
  Where the faithful all stand
In awe of Nimrod's sceptre

II.

The Chaldean immigrants
Full on grist,
Multiplied, increasing without restraint
Smelting the old regalia into craven idols

They amputated my knees
But I can still feel my legs
    Inflexible,
I buckle under the change

But they shall not take the standard of Ur

Alive my friends
We stand free

Preserved by sand
    In death
We will not be forgotten

Chaldeans
for Moni

we are the spore stars
watching the planets
charting the horizon
finding patterns in all things
    calculating their
        width
                and
      depth

we are the Chaldeans
underwriters of the heavenly war
debating on the number string
mapping out the luminous orbs
    Soma constitutes
                the greater
                    part
            of our geometry

we anoint with semen
as the spermatozoa swims in an array
fanning out like tendrils
    veins in the gothic arch

we are the apostles of the eternal glory
winners on the astroplane
lying on our backs in bliss
accepting the throb and thrust
within the plasmatic ocean
                of
                the never ending
                womb

for the void is pleasant
and love is the best thing
in any world

and we are eternity
in insemination
holding all the answers

we are the Brahmans
princes of the cosmic waste
that primordial gland that issues chaos
throughout existence
     pushing and expanding the universe
           through pulse
               and
             penetration

o Great Potential, touching us with glimpses
of your splendour
we are the righteous tribesman
seeking out the menstrual cycle of the lunar
houses

for creation is our highest act
as we reap from the broken vale
in that place where there is no time

we are the harvesters of wisdom
marked by apostolic succession
phosphorescent Christian halos
and Phrygian caps

the Aryan council
in the darkened night
where neon mandalas glow in the fray

we are the sailors on the event horizon
where our third eye is tethered
to the sacred gem
the sephirot of nothing

the priestly elect
standing above judgement
and the laws of average men
    with our days spent in stasis
        swimming in the ocean
           of
      GOD

YHWE

the sun rises on the temple mount
where the threshing floor is covered in blood

the sacred ark holds her fiery heart
    she, who speaks in jealous tongues
but does not feel jealousy
searing the skin of those whose intentions are not
    pure

for she will strike like a black widow
    her hand around the neck
of the faithful lover
who ignores her admonition

the old Aaronites,
    priests of levitation, are afraid to speak her
    name
whispering it under their breath
permutating its letters

they whisper:
YHWE

3+3+3=9

I will ask the elements to bring you spring
a bouquet wrapped in your essence
cellophane that remembers where we've been

and who we used to be
when we lived before this time
in lands situated on bluffs by the sea

we flew over green covered highlands
now we have to settle for making love
and the faint feeling, resembling a memory

we will ally ourselves with the forces of nature
travel within the wind
ride bareback on the storm

drink from the rain
catch hail from heaven
and decipher the secrets of frogs

toast from the river's flow
bring salutations to the trees
and match the vibrations of rocks

for three is the mark of the wind
as God is that which decides between
    my thoughts and dreams

    three mothers
talked about in days of threes
for it takes nine months to make a baby

Tender in the Age of Fury

o darling, I will kiss your belly
home to creation
house to all that is holy

never severing the thing that binds
        the truest of truths
that was revealed to those of us who stop time

        for a day of God
is but centuries to the commuting consumer
and you are my fellow traveller on this cosmic ride

and there will be others
who will follow the magic dust left on the trails we paved
they are our children's children

generations from now
they will know us
by the enchantments we create

the immortality offered to those
who dare reach up to heaven
and sculpt the everlasting art

are you afraid? do you dare?
trash it all and burn the sheets
as I pour everything I am into you

The Carbon Age

Poems: 2011-2014

The Admonition to My Children

The madness of my forefathers has called to haunt
    like a bony knuckle
tapping on my door
its authority has my house surrounded
     facing its warrant, I have no place to go

I cannot outrun this centuries old apparition
    its spindly appendages
crawls into my ear when I'm sleeping
thrusting me into waking dreams
     the horrible breath, whispering deceit and lies

I have no reason to humour it
    it's like a tumour that grows
pushing aside my healthy brain
     making room by the fire to taunt me
while keeping me company

The insanity of my ancestors has come to call
    bringing with it the turmoil that came before me
memories of those who could not get out of bed
who tried to bar their windows with whores and hash
who washed in booze, or preferred not eating
    to the fast end
     of a bullet
          in the temple
             from a gun

The Carbon Age

I am a private world
the root of my own age
born into carbon
meticulously arranged

For You

These are the portions I have cut
    a diamond for your finger
    sublime planes
to reflect your splendour

This is the collection of roses
    picked for you
as the thorns drew the blood
that my heart continually pushed
dripping down into the soil
that I mulched with loving care
to prepare a shady place for you to sit
    A garden I will tend
    lush vines and dew laden ferns
sown into a wreath
to lay upon your shoulders

A fixed heel
cobbled by artisans
    How you love your shoes
I hear them clack, on the stones I have set
masonry that broke my back
laying the foundation to the house of your leisure
where I wove the carpets
that cushion your feet
worshiping your faults
as strengths beyond measure
as you lay bare on satin sheets
while I make you coffee
after your late sleep

How I wish
    this was good enough
      for you

Brandon Pitts

In My Hour of Death

In my hour of death
do not let me cling to this life
but allow me to pass with grace
leaving this realm of conditional love

Do not mourn for this spirit
who has grown tired
but accept the passing of one
who understands the Father
    infinite space
        and is not afraid of ghosts

Foreign Campaigns

Occidental expeditions
to lands of firm packed spice
bricks of black tea
and nights of lovers
    whose touch is understood

They lay on mats
with customs I cannot understand
misinterpreted gestures
intelligence and personal subtleties
    lost in the difference of language

We lie
yearning for experience
loving the exotic
as my hand moves gently down her thigh
    bridging the variance within the night

but those campaigns
beyond our borders
where the skirmish
brought painful bounties
    were only the beginning
      of my exile
        from the mundane

Creature

there is a creature on our roof
reminding me how much I miss you
how my heart is breaking
how I've never felt the tenderness and closeness
that I have shared while holding you
how I have the deepest
most oppressed feeling
that I am not only losing my life's mate, but my
    best friend
I'm sorry I haven't contacted you
it's not that I don't want to
but if I keep moving
riding my bike around town
visiting people or staying busy
I feel no pain

but sitting here, drinking coffee alone
listening to the creature scratch at the shingles
I have to admit my sorrow
I weep because I miss you and still love you
not even as much as I did
but maybe
a little more

The Labours of
Spartacus Baptist

for Senator Bernie Sanders

The Labours of Spartacus Baptist

Labour of the first

Planes flew from the east
on the day he was born
leaving chem trails
from horizon
to temple mount

Knowing that a new Baptist had emerged among
    the serfs
a multi-faced behemoth
rose out of the halls of justice
with breasts of a woman
and groin of a man

The pope and president
each took turns
riding on its back

Lo Spartacus Baptist
a mere babe in a trough
wash your loincloth in the gutters
of thy lord's streets

for you shall answer to no one
on this imperial journey
    from first imprint to death
lead us along the Pall Mall
    to serenity
where we can raise our children in peace

Labour of the second

Spartacus Baptist speaks for the people
enemy of the state
    he calls for truth in the senate
and justice in the mirrored halls
    He walks upon pavement
through the streets of Tokyo, New York, and Rome
calling for all to share in earth's bounty

The Centurions will chase Spartacus Baptist
merchants will deny him credit
and the law will burden him with their fascination
    They will disallow him the privilege of slavery
leaving him but one option: the Cross

Sit with Spartacus Baptist on the first eve of many
    suppers
see him bless the bread and carve the roast
    No child shall be denied as he reaches into
    his basket
turning hardship into wine and misfortune into a
    hot meal

*Let me tell you the **Parable of the Once Righteous Man**,*
sayeth Spartacus Baptist:

A righteous man was once approached by strange
    spirits in a dream
who told him that Caesar was going to impose a tax on
    the act of communication
a pence for every word he did speak
and this tax could not be paid in cash or he would incur
    a stiff penalty
it would be easier to let Caesar's agents handle the
    transaction for him
charging only a small courtesy fee
I accept your generous offer, sayeth the Once Righteous
    Man, without realising that he'd been charged five
    pence just to talk

And the disciples sat in silence.

Labour of the third

See Spartacus Baptist standing at the baptismal font
on the shores of the Rivers Commerce
washing sins from the brows of the toilers

Mud on hands will now cleanse the skin
instead of staining savage pores
    Happiness, sayeth Spartacus Baptist
is not a spoil but a right
So I shall relay to you
*the **Parable of the House of Trust***

An old Scrivener had amassed a meagre pension in a
        house of trust
for each time he'd deposit one of Caesar's shillings, the
        teller would take a haypence
Every time the Scrivener withdrew his money, the
        teller would skim a wholepence
This confused the Scrivener
        for the master of the house of trust had insured
        him a preferred rate of interest
Since the Scrivener had been depositing shillings on a
        perpetual basis
his money had the appearance of growth
but in reality it had been shrinking
        This was compounded by the magical appearance
        of paper money, produced by the bank, and given
        to the Scrivener and others when they withdrew
        their deposits

Then came the day where the Scrivener put aside his
    toil to relish his old age
but these were the days when metal coin and backed
    bank notes had become passé and almost illegal
money was now exchanged through a system of debits,
    each incurring its own fee and it had the ability to
    purchase things without a physical exchange of gold

But where had they buried the Scrivener's coin? asked
    the Baptist

Spartacus Baptist's disciples could not answer this
    dilemma

Labour of the forth

See Spartacus Baptist press tender lips
to the foreheads of babes
assigning the Angels Protectorate
to their souls as they sleep

so they grow up free
and safe from the numbing Dajjal
and the spirits of control
who steal their souls in the night

Tell us Spartacus Baptist
tell us how we are not really free
but slaves to the engines
of Herod and Minos

thrown down into the bowels of destruction
held back from the God given well
Tell us Spartacus, before they toss you into the pit
with the Nazarene

Labour of the fifth

See Spartacus Baptist tend to the elderly
lifting the ladle of soup to lips
cracked by the stress of days
spent in the never ending cycle of toil

See him decipher the capital codex
preaching on the floor of the money hall
shouting over the growl of Moloch
and the grind of the exchange

See him part the sea of slaves:
those who long for freedom
and those who believe they are free
      Lo Spartacus Baptist!

Now let me tell you the **Parable of the Duck Hunters,**
sayeth he:

Six men embarked upon a duck hunting trip, some
      years after the turn of the last century
      The ducks had all flown north for the season
so all that was left to hunt were sheep

This was easy to do
for the six men were used to operating in the shadows,
      places where deposits were considered a liability
      and loans an asset used to create more money by
      reaching into a magical bottomless basket

There were rumours that these six men were impervious
      to death, and had achieved immortality by living
      off the blood of the innocent, creating poverty and
      war in the process

Brandon Pitts

How can you trust in God, asked Spartacus Baptist,
when garlic and the Cross cannot protect you?

And the disciples wondered what the Baptist meant

94

Labour of the sixth

These are the provisions of Spartacus Baptist
heralding yet another new year
where the weak shall inherit peace
and base human rights:

No child shall feel the grind

The toiler shall not labour but one-seventh of their week
        for the baron

One soul's greed shall not burden that of another

No persons shall lean with old age
having given their backs to aid
in another person's commerce

Christmas shall no longer be a day of financial reckoning
but a reminder that each day
is a holiday worth remembering
for this Baptist tells us that we are alive
and a day of respite is a holiday for the slave

And the disciples argued among themselves
some feeling that the Baptist had gone too far

Labour of the seventh

See Spartacus Baptist heal the sick
making provisions for the poor
removing the sorcerer's leech from the skin of the
    elderly

A craftsman by trade
he ushered the lake to flow like a river
washing them out from the factory
where toil meant a creditors wage

    But then it rained for eighty nights
suffering cold
praying for the means
to buy heat

His disciples abandoned him when
vegetables became more expensive than grain
processed in a strange mill
where horse power meant light

Spartacus Baptist did not die on the cross
but laid his burden down
while trying to pinch salt
from the Sea of Galilee

They dismembered him
to pay his bills
and the local magnate
sold tickets in the coliseum
as the women danced around his severed head

Lo Spartacus Baptist!

Pontius Pilate

I hath abandoned peace
for violence

nurture for remorse

given up on love
only to love the stripper of destruction

rejected into acceptance of drink
and the false high of worn concepts

I abandoned her . . . for you

and you abandoned me
for him

put aside convention
to eat from the plate of life

and walk through the houses of fate
before I break
    into
      a
           thousand
                unfixable
    pieces

But... the spirits doth guide me
    the devil approved when I strayed
      and the Lord of Hosts forgave me my
    blasphemy

for I was tender . . . in the age of fury

God Bless!

97

Thank You

First and foremost, I'd like to thank Mosaic Press. Terry Barker for believing Mosaic was a good home for my work and for getting behind the book; and Howard Aster for believing in me.

To my earliest supporters: Jasmine D'Costa, Norman Cristofoli of Labour of Love Poetry Magazine, and Cheryl Antao-Xavier of IOWI (In Our Words Inc.) Thank you!

Thanks to all who booked me for poetry readings and helped to promote me: Nik Beat – RIP (CIUT 89.5 fm), Alana P. Cook, Margaret Code, Valentino Assenza, Josh Smith and Stephen Humphrey (The Art Bar), Lizzie Violet (Cabaret Noir – the Beautiful and the Damned – Lipstik Indie), Creative James Dewer (Hot Sauced Words), Phillip Cairns, David Bateman, Duncan Armstrong and D.M. Moore (the Beautiful and the Damned), Brenda Clews (Urban Gallery – general promotor and inspiration for video poems), Art on the Danforth, the Keep Toronto Reading Festival and the Toronto Reference Library, Helen Walsh and Natalie Kertes (Diaspora Dialogues), Madison Shadwell (the Central), Liz Worth and Jordan Tannahill (Video Fag), Jan McIntyre (Loose Leaf Poets), Shawna Marie Andrews (the Cafe Connection), Ivy Reiss and Elka Ruth Enola (Lit Cafe), Sherry Isaac (Prana Coffee Presents: A Night of Poetry and Prose and Noah's Hotel in Nuestadt), Duane Kirby Jensen (Everett Poetry Night), Chele Eva Armstrong, Thom Davis, and Dobbie Reese Norris (Bellingham Poetry Night), Russell Carrick (Couth Buzzard), Jordan Fry (Niagara Literary Festival), Stella and Graham Ducker (the Stellar Literary

Festival), Origo Books, Tom Fischer (the Sonic Cafe, the Last Temptation and the Record Vault), Hainzle Malcolm (the Solstice Cafe), Farzana Doctor (the Brockton Writer's Series), the Supermarket, Sabrina Grafton (Index Art Festival), David Burga and Robert Campbell (R&R Books), Bunny Iskov (the Rivoli and the Ontario Poetry Society), and Leo Paradela and Luciano Iacobelli (Q-Space).

Thanks to fellow poets Stedmond Pardy, Susan Munro as well as folks like Anita Keller, Mary Lou Pachel, Laura L'Rock, Paris Black and others who have hosted poetry salons and after hours parties, inviting poets to get up and read at rock concerts, parking lots, etc, where poetry thrived at all hours in Toronto. Thank you to Saskia van Tetering, Topaz Amber Dawn, and Gerald Pitts for proofreading and Abby Amjad. Also thanks to Joan Sutcliffe and Honey Novick and the Butler's Pantry crowd.

Thank you to Gilchrist Pitts for help with graphics, making event fliers and touching up photos.

Thank you Monica Durante for being a muse.

Special thanks to the Daughter of Irma, muse to many of these poems.

Special thanks to Jennifer Hosein for being a great friend through the rough times that accompanied the composition of these poems and lending her amazing artistic talents to the cover painting and author photo.

Acknowledgements

An early version of "The Doctor of Theology" was previously published in *Labour of Love Poetry Magazine* Vol. 38 Winter 2014 ISSN 1192-621X

An early version of "Zul Qarnain" was published in *Randomly Accessed Poetics* poetry anthology, "Heart Splatters Into Significance" Penhead Press 2014 ISBN 978-09887938-2-8. (This was Penhead Press' first print edition.) The poem also came out in the digital edition, Issue #4, ASIN B00HGF80HC December 2013.

"Nimrod" was previously published in the magazine, *The Raven's Claw* – October 2012
An early version of "In My Hour of Death" was previously published in the magazine *Labour of Love* – issue #36, Winter 2012.
"Magdalene" was previously published in the anthology, *The Courtney Park Connection* – In Our Words Inc, and the digital version of *Randomly Accessed Poetic's* anthology, "Heart Splatters Into Significance."

"A Poem for AQ," "Lot" and, "Hammurabi" were previously published in the collection, *Pressure to Sing* – In Our Words Inc. December 2011 ISBN 978-1-926926-11-7

"Hammurabi" was first published by the Brooklin Poetry Society in their anthology, *On My Poppy*, November 2011, ISBN 978-0-9866539-1-9

"A Poem for AQ" was first published in the magazine *Labour of Love* – issue #33, Winter 2010.

The third section of "Lot" was previously published in the magazine *Labour of Love* – issue #34, Summer 2011.
"Lot" was also published in an annotated edition by bojit Press.

Biography

Brandon Pitts is the author of the popular poetry collection *Pressure to Sing* (IOWI, 2012).

Known for subverting gospel and scripture to create political allegories, Brandon first came onto the Toronto lit scene in 2010 with the short story "The BC Crib", published in the anthology *Canadian Voices Volume II*. In 2011, he was inducted into the prestigious Diaspora Dialogues as an "Emerging Voice" for fiction, followed by the novel *Puzzle of Murders* (Bookland Press, 2011) and the production of three plays.

List of Publications by Brandon Pitts

Books

Pressure To Sing IOWI (In Our Words Inc.) Jan. 2012

Killcreek – a play IOWI (In Our Words Inc.) Jun. 2013

Puzzle of Murders Bookland Press, Nov. 2011

The Annotated Lot bojit Press, Jan. 2015

Anthologies

The Courtney Park Connection – Prose and Poetry Edited by Brandon Pitts, IOWI (In Our Words Inc.) Aug. 2013

TOK 7 – Reading the New Toronto Zephyr Press, May 2012

Canadian Voices II Bookland Press, Nov. 2010

Randomly Accessed Poetics – Heart Splatters Into Significance Penhead Press, April 2014

On My Poppy Poetry Anthology, Broklin Poetry Society, Nov. 2011

The Bracelet Charm Short Story Anthology, Volume 5, #40. *Conceit Magazine*, Summer 2009

Plays

Killcreek Performed for two weeks at the Randolph Theatre, Toronto Fringe, Toronto ON, Jul. 2013

Johanna Performed for one night (sold out) at Montgomery's Inn, Toronto ON, May 24th, 2013

One Night Performed for two weeks at the George Ignatieff Theatre, Toronto Fringe, Toronto ON, Jul. 2012

Magazines and Musical Works

Labour Of Love Poetry Magazine, Volume 38, Winter 2014

The New Music Concert Series Classical composer, Adam Scime used Brandon's poem "Loved Creatures" for his "Earth and Air II," along with poems by James Joyce and Ezra Pound. It was performed Feb. 3rd, 2013 at the Betty Oliphant Theatre in Toronto.

Spewgore – Faceplant (CD) At the beginning of the song, "Set To Fail", Brandon can be heard reciting a short section of his epic poem, "The Apocalypse of Weeks." Nov. 2013

Labour Of Love Poetry Magazine, Volume 35, Winter 2012 (Brandon also shot the cover photo)

The Raven's Call Magazine, A Dark Place Publication, Oct. 2012

Labour Of Love Poetry Magazine, Volume 34, Summer 2011

Labour Of Love Poetry Magazine, Volume 33, Winter 2011

Quick Brown Fox Literary Blog and Newsletter, Sept. 2008

Emancipation – Roslyn Brown (CD) Brandon wrote the lyrics to the song, "The Siren."

List of Poetry Readings, Literary Festivals, Performed Plays, and Esential Appearances by Brandon Pitts

Index Art Festival
Index Elementary School, July 24th 2014
Index Washington, USA

Lizzie Violet's Cabaret Noir
Central Tavern, July 18th
Toronto Ontario, 2014

Art Bar
(With A.F. Moritz)
Black Swan Tavern, July 13th, 2014
Toronto Ontario, Canada

Best Originals
(Winner – Best Poet)
Hirut on the Danforth, July 2nd, 2014
Toronto Ontario, Canada

Urban Gallery – June-bug Romp
(With bill bissett, David Bateman, Kirk DeMatas, and Phillip Cairns)
June 28th, 2014
Toronto Ontario, Canada

Poetry Night
Bellingham Public Library, May 12th, 2014
Bellingham Washington, USA

Everett Poetry Night
Cafe Zippy, March 6th, 2014
Everett Washington, USA

Kids and Caffeine
(With Clinton Feron and Selassie I Soldier)
Solstice Cafe, October 12th, 2013
Seattle Washington, USA

Couth Buzzard
September 19th, 2013
Seattle Washington, USA

Killcreek – a play
(Toronto Fringe)
Friday, July 5, 2013, Sunday, July 7, 2013,
Monday, July 8, 2013, Wednesday, July 10, 2013
Thursday, July 11, 2013, Saturday, July 13, 2013
Sunday, July 14, 2013
Randolph Theatre
Toronto Ontario, Canada

Johanna – a play
Humber River Shakespeare Co's Sonnet Show
May 24th, 2013
Montgomery Inn
Etobicoke Ontario, Canada

Lizzie Violet's Caberet Noir
(With Melting Pot and Bella Fox)
Q-Space, April 14th, 2013
Toronto Ontario, Canada

Video Fag
With Salt Circle (Liz Worth and Sam Cooper), Nik
Beat, and Jacqueline Valencia
Kensington Market, March 16th, 2013
Toronto Ontario, Canada

Hot Sauced Words
Black Swan Tavern, February 21st 2013
Toronto Ontario

Loose Leaf Poets & Writer's
Fogarty's Pub, January 7th, 2013
Toronto Ontario, Canada

Q-Space
(With Greg "Ritalin" Frankson and Vanessa McGowan)
December, 16th 2012
Toronto, Ontario, Canada

The Beautiful and the Damned
(With Nina Arsenault and Ellie Anderson)
Zelda's, March 8th 2012,
Toronto Ontario, Canada